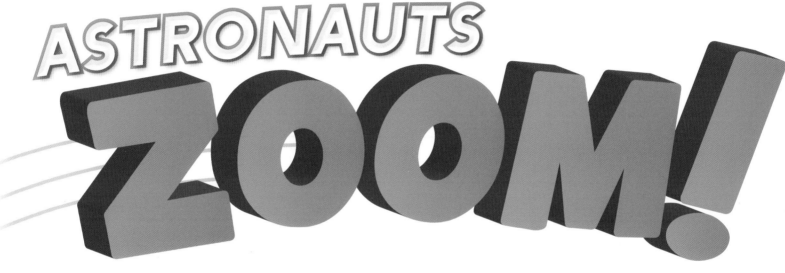

ASTRONAUTS ZOOM!

An Astronaut Alphabet

PERSNICKETY PRESS

Design by Brian Scott Sockin
and Shan Stumpf

ISBN: 978-1-943978-50-2

10 9 8 7 6 5 4 3 2 1

PERSNICKETY
PRESS

Published by Persnickety Press
An imprint of WunderMill, Inc.
321 Glen Echo Ln, Ste. C
Cary, NC 27518
www.persnickety-press.com

WunderMill
www.wundermillbooks.com

For Bona, Simbo, and Asher, so you will always reach for the stars

Very special thanks to the astronauts from around the world who have advanced human knowledge and achievement by living and working on the International Space Station, and to all the people whose work on Earth makes astronauts' work in space possible

Extra thanks to Daniel Huot, NASA Public Affairs

ASTRONAUTS ZOOM!

An Astronaut Alphabet

By Deborah Lee Rose

Author of *Scientists Get Dressed* and
Coauthor of *Beauty and the Beak*

PERSNICKETY PRESS

Day and night,
astronauts *zoom*
around Earth on the
International Space Station.

What do astronauts
do while they zoom?

A

Astronauts awake **to start their day!**

B

Astronauts brush their teeth.

C

Astronauts
all help
clean up.

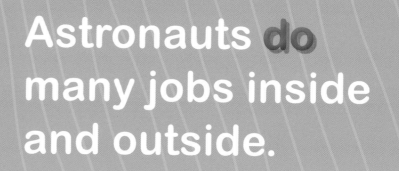

D

Astronauts do many jobs inside and outside.

E

Astronauts exercise every day.

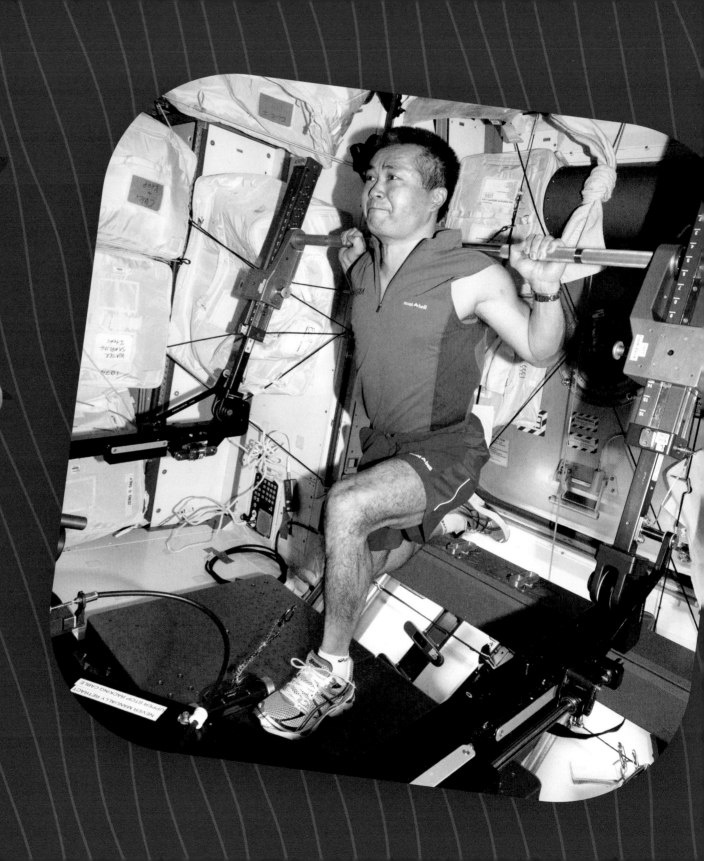

F

Astronauts float!

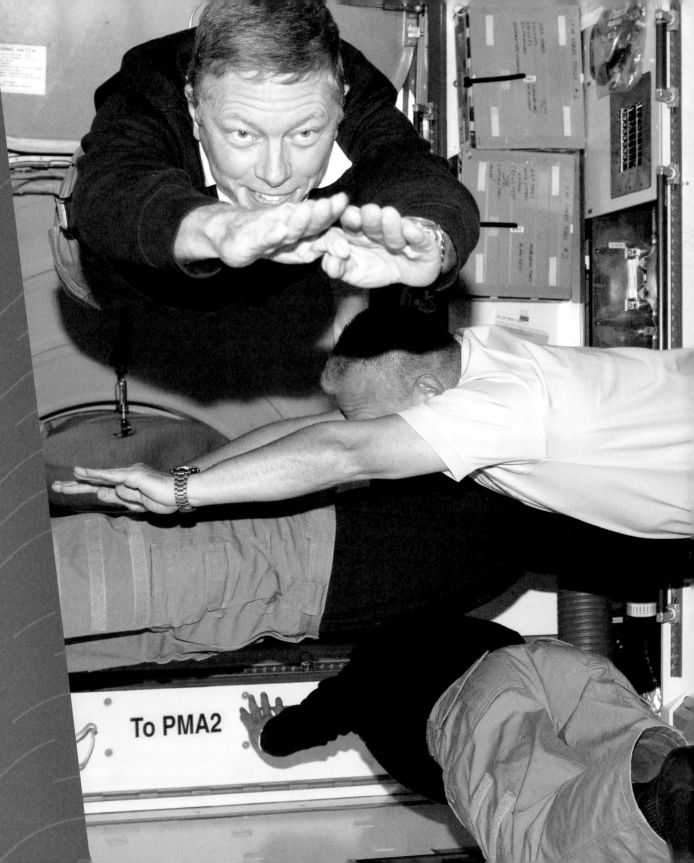

To PMA2

G

H

Astronauts **go**
on spacewalks
wearing spacesuits
and **helmets**.

Astronauts investigate science questions.

J

Astronauts **juggle** fruit **for fun.**

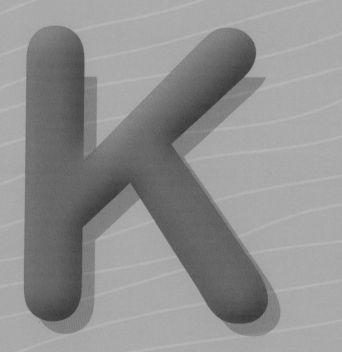

Astronauts kick soccer balls.

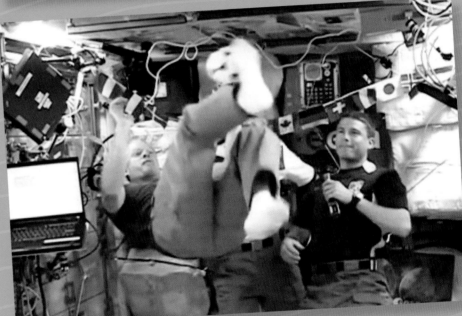

L M
N O

Astronauts **love** to **make** pizza— but **need** a space **oven**!

P

Astronauts **play** music and sing together.

Q

Astronauts have **quiet** time.

R

Astronauts read!

S

Astronauts shampoo **their hair.**

T

Astronauts talk **to people back on Earth.**

U

Astronauts go **upside** down!

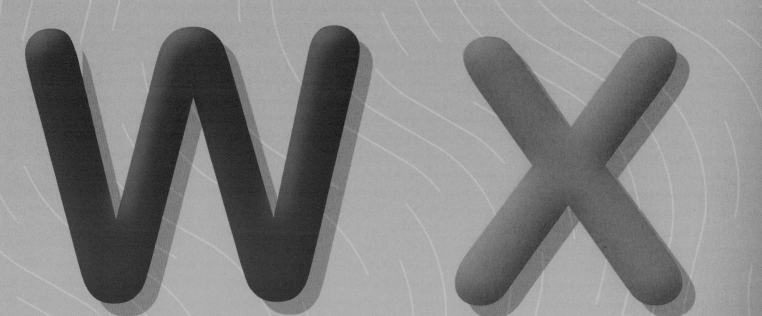

V W X

Astronauts view Earth from space. "**WOW**!!!" they exclaim.

Y

Astronauts yawn and get ready for bed.

Z

Astronauts zoom,
zipped in for the night.

ASTRONAUTS ZOOM! FROM A TO Z

Aa — Astronauts *awake* to start their day!

When astronauts wake up, you might be sound asleep on Earth. When it's dark outside the International Space Station, astronauts soon see sunrise. The station orbits around our planet—and astronauts see a new sunrise—every 90 minutes!

Bb — Astronauts *brush* their teeth.

Astronauts brush their teeth with their lips closed, to keep toothpaste and water bubbles from floating through the International Space Station. They spit their toothpaste into a towel or washcloth when they're done.

Cc — Astronauts all help *clean* up.

Inside the International Space Station, astronauts vacuum and wipe up often. This helps keep all kinds of equipment from getting clogged or broken. Astronauts make as little trash as possible, and recycle as much as they can.

Dd — Astronauts *do* many jobs inside and outside.

Astronauts work as a team. Their computers are some of the most important tools they use inside the International Space Station. Outside the station, they can ride on the huge robotic arm to do science experiments and make engineering repairs.

Ee — Astronauts *exercise* every day.

On Earth, gravity helps keep you strong by pulling on your muscles and bones. In microgravity on the International Space Station, astronauts' bodies can get weak. Astronauts stay strong and fit by exercising every day.

Ff — Astronauts *float*!

Astronauts don't need chairs on the International Space Station. They float. Sitting, standing, and moving in microgravity are very different than on Earth. That's why astronauts train a lot on Earth—including in a giant pool—to be able to work in space.

Gg / Hh — Astronauts *go* on spacewalks wearing spacesuits and *helmets*.

Astronauts go outside the International Space Station from a special "airlock" section. This is sealed off from the rest of the station. Outside, they do engineering work and science experiments, sometimes standing on the station's robotic arm.

Spacesuits, or EMUs (Extravehicular Mobility Units), give astronauts air to breathe and water to drink. Helmets with gold visors and gloves with fingertip warmers also protect astronauts from burning solar rays, extreme cold, and flying particles.

Thin water tubes in their long underwear keep astronauts cool when they're working hard on a long spacewalk. (They also wear adult diapers under their suits.) Strong tethers, like ropes, keep astronauts from floating away into space.

Ii — Astronauts *investigate* science questions.

Astronauts do experiments on the International Space Station, to explore things like how much water and light plants need away from Earth, and how living in microgravity for many months affects people. Students even design some of the experiments!

Jj — Astronauts *juggle* fruit for fun.

Fun is a little different on the International Space Station. In space, astronauts can juggle many more pieces than on Earth. In microgravity, objects don't fall all the way to the floor. So until an astronaut catches them, the objects stay up in the air.

Kk — Astronauts *kick* soccer balls.

On the International Space Station, you can kick a soft soccer ball while somersaulting like a gymnast! If you play baseball, you can bat and catch your own hit. The ball just floats until an astronaut catches it.

Ll / Mm / Nn / Oo — Astronauts *love* to *make* pizza— but *need* a space *oven*.

Tasty foods, including from astronauts' own countries, are important on the International Space Station. Astronauts heat pizzas in an oven with small sections, not big open racks. They even eat while their pizzas are floating!

Pp — Astronauts *play* music and sing together.

Playing music and singing help astronauts feel less far away from Earth. Musical instruments sound the same on the International Space Station as on Earth, but some instruments are harder to play when they and astronauts are floating.

Qq — Astronauts have *quiet* time.

Astronauts need time to relax. They watch movies or sports happening on Earth, like the Olympics, or make craft projects like models of the International Space Station. They all think about what they'll do when they get back to Earth.

Rr — Astronauts *read*!

Astronauts read books, articles, and messages—in different languages— from their families, friends, coworkers, and others. Astronauts need to read lots of science and engineering information to keep the International Space Station working.

Ss — Astronauts *shampoo* their hair.

A shower or bath uses too much water to have on the International Space Station. And even single water drops float in microgravity. Astronauts squirt on a little water and rinseless shampoo, rub them in, then dry their hair with a towel.

Tt — Astronauts *talk* to people back on Earth.

Astronauts can talk to people on Earth through computer phone calls, video streaming, ham radio, and more. From the International Space Station, astronauts speak about life and work in space to kids and adults around the world.

Uu — Astronauts go *upside* down!

At first, astronauts' senses get confused about up and down on the International Space Station. Some say they feel like they're hanging like a bat! But after astronauts adapt to microgravity, they can do what they need to do in any direction.

Vv / Ww / Xx — Astronauts *view* Earth from space. "*WOW*!!!" they *exclaim*.

Astronauts say that seeing Earth from the International Space Station changes their lives. They see hurricanes swirling, volcanoes erupting, and lights going on wherever it's night. They can also see things like our Milky Way galaxy more clearly.

Yy — Astronauts *yawn* and get ready for bed.

In microgravity, astronauts zip themselves into sleeping bags, so their bodies won't float around bumping things. At astronaut bedtime, outside the International Space Station might be totally light, and you might be wide awake on Earth!

Zz — Astronauts *zoom*, zipped in for the night.

Day and night, the International Space Station and its astronauts fly superfast— at 17,500 miles (28,000 kilometers) per hour. Astronauts mostly sleep in their own cabins, but find extra sleeping spaces when more astronauts are onboard.

Explore more about astronauts and space at https://www.nasa.gov

HOW DO ASTRONAUTS PRACTICE FOR WORKING ON THE INTERNATIONAL SPACE STATION?

Astronauts from many countries have helped make amazing STEM advances. Before they launch into space, they train here on Earth.

One of the most important things astronauts practice is suiting up. Spacesuit safety experts on Earth help astronauts put on ("don") and take off ("doff") their spacesuits over and over again. This teaches astronauts how to get dressed—and help each other get dressed—for real spacewalks on the space station. Boots, helmets, and gloves must all fit perfectly.

Astronauts do major spacewalk training in a giant pool. At NASA's Neutral Buoyancy Laboratory, they wear spacesuits to work underwater on a space station replica. In the pool, astronauts can practice making engineering repairs, doing experiments, floating upside down, and rescuing each other quickly.

ABOUT THE INTERNATIONAL SPACE STATION

- Astronauts have zoomed, lived and worked on the International Space Station since November 2, 2000. In total, astronauts from at least 19 countries have flown billions of miles on the space station.

- The International Space Station is the third brightest object in our sky, after the Sun and Moon. Even without a telescope, people on Earth can see the station zooming through space 250 miles (400 kilometers) above Earth's surface.

- The space station is the size of a football field! On Earth, with full gravity, the station would weigh nearly 1,000,000 pounds (420,000 kilograms).

- About once every 90 minutes, or 16 times in every 24 hours, the International Space Station completes an orbit around Earth. The space station travels extremely fast—17,500 miles (28,000 kilometers) per hour.

- While the station is zooming so fast it is falling in free fall towards Earth. But at such high speed the space station's path follows the curve of Earth's shape, so the station stays in orbit and never hits Earth.

- Photos and videos show astronauts, and objects, floating on the International Space Station. How do they float, since they are actually being pulled on by 90 percent of Earth's gravity?

- Astronauts and objects appear to float because they are also falling in free fall towards Earth. Since they fall at the same speed as the space station, they look like they are floating.

HOW CAN I TURN MY CLASSROOM, MULTIPURPOSE ROOM, ENTIRE SCHOOL, LIBRARY, OR HOME AREA INTO AN "INTERNATIONAL SPACE STATION" ENVIRONMENT?

- Set up a "cupola" reading area, that looks like where astronauts see out the International Space Station windows.

- Make "windows" from photos of what astronauts see from space, and gather space books like *Astronauts Zoom!* Find space station photos of Earth online including in the NASA Image and Video Library at https://images.nasa.gov.

- Compare astronauts' day and night on the International Space Station to kids' on Earth. Use photos, art, writing, graphs, models, or whatever you like to show how they are the same and different.

- Make and/or hang flags of countries whose astronauts have worked together on the International Space Station including United States, Canada, United Kingdom, Russia, Italy, South Korea, Japan, Belgium, Spain, France, Netherlands, Sweden, Brazil, Denmark, Kazakhstan, Malaysia, South Africa, Germany, and United Arab Emirates.

- Design and make your own International Space Station expedition patch (like astronauts do) to wear or display.

- Set up experiments to do where you are, or design experiments that astronauts might do in space.

- Have a space station pizza party. Make or order in real pizzas, or make paper collage pizzas.

- Exercise the way astronauts do on the International Space Station, by running, biking, and/or lifting weights.

- Try "space" sports and fun activities, like playing soccer with a soft ball and juggling.

- Make International Space Station models from toy bricks or recycled materials.

- Make a video "from space" and/or write letters or emails "from space."

ASTRONAUTS ZOOM! WORDS

- adapt
- airlock
- astronaut
- cupola
- curve
- doff
- don
- EMU (Extravehicular Mobility Unit)
- engineering
- equipment
- erupting
- expedition
- experiments
- float
- free fall
- galaxy
- gravity
- ham radio
- helmet
- hurricanes
- International Space Station
- investigate
- launch
- microgravity
- Milky Way
- NASA
- Neutral Buoyancy Lab
- Olympics
- onboard
- orbit
- particles
- patch
- recycle
- replica
- robotic arm
- science
- senses
- solar rays
- somersaulting
- space
- spacesuit
- spacewalk
- technology
- telescope
- tethers
- training
- vacuum
- video streaming
- visor
- volcanoes

NGSS HIGHLIGHTS

Connections to Nature of Science: Science is a Human Endeavor, Scientific Investigations Use a Variety of Methods, Science Knowledge is Based on Empirical Evidence, Science is a Way of Knowing / **Connections to Engineering, Technology, and Applications of Science:** Influence of Science, Engineering, and Technology on Society and the Natural World/Science and Engineering Practices: Asking Questions and Defining Problems

AUTHOR BIO

Deborah Lee Rose is the internationally published author of *Astronauts Zoom!* and *Scientists Get Dressed* (winner of the national DeBary Award for Outstanding Science Books for Children), and coauthor with Jane Veltkamp of *Beauty and the Beak: How Science, Technology, and a 3D-Printed Beak Rescued a Bald Eagle* (winner of the AAAS/Subaru SB&F Prize for Excellence in Science Books and the Bank Street College Cook Prize for Best STEM Picture Book), all three STEM books published by Persnickety Press/WunderMill Books).

She is also the author of the beloved and classic books *The Twelve Days of Kindergarten*, *The Twelve Days of Winter*, *Jimmy the Joey*, and *Into the A, B, Sea: An Ocean Alphabet* which has sold more than a quarter million copies. Her books have been included in language arts collections in the United States, Canada, the United Kingdom, France, and South Africa, and published in multiple languages. Deborah was senior science writer for UC Berkeley's renowned Lawrence Hall of Science, where she worked on many groundbreaking STEM education projects, including several funded by NASA. She directed communications for the ALA/AASL honored, NSF-funded STEM education website *howtosmile.org*. A graduate of Cornell University, Deborah lives in Silver Spring, Maryland and speaks to conferences, book festivals, schools, and libraries across the country. *www.deborahleerose.com*

ASTRONAUTS IN THE BOOK
(in order of appearance)

- David Wolf (cover, do jobs—outside)/US
- Drew Feustel (day and night, play music)/US
- Nick Hague (awake)/US
- Christina Koch (awake, go on spacewalks)/US
- Anne McClain (awake, investigate)/US
- David Saint-Jacques (awake)/Canada
- Kimiya Yui (brush)/Japan
- Sandra Magnus (clean)/US
- Victor Glover (do jobs—inside)/US
- Koichi Wakata (exercise)/Japan
- Michael Fossum (float, practice—underwater)/US
- Ronald Garan (float)/US
- Douglas Hurley (float)/US
- John Herrington (go on spacewalks)/US
- Jessica Meir (go on spacewalks, investigate, practice—spacesuit)/US
- Scott Kelly (juggle)/US
- Alexander Gerst (kick)/Germany
- Steven Swanson (kick)/US
- Reid Wiseman (kick, practice—waving in pool)/US
- Joseph Acaba (pizza)/US
- Randolph Bresnik (pizza)/US
- Paolo Nespoli (pizza)/Italy
- Scott Tingle (play music)/US

- Tracy Caldwell Dyson (quiet, upside down)/US
- Joan Higginbotham (read)/US
- Sunita Williams (read)/US
- Timothy Peake (read)/UK
- Karen Nyberg (shampoo)/US
- Jack Fischer (talk)/US
- Peggy Whitson (talk)/US
- Dorothy Metcalf-Lindenburger (upside down)/US
- Stephanie Wilson (upside down)/US
- Naoko Yamazaki (upside down)/Japan
- Samantha Cristoforetti (view, yawn)/Italy
- Daniel Tani (zoom, zipped)/US
- Robert Satcher (practice—checking glove)/US
- Robert Curbeam (go on spacewalks)/US
- Christer Fuglesang (go on spacewalks)/Sweden

PHOTO CREDITS

All photos from NASA except: brushing teeth, ESA/JAXA/NASA; reading in cupola, ESA/NASA; taking photos, ESA/NASA; astronaut and divers under water, NASA/*Houston Chronicle*, Smiley N. Pool; astronaut being helped with spacesuit pants, James Blair/NASA